# COCAINE

## DRUGS AREN'T THE ONLY THINGS THAT PEOPLE CAN BE ADDICTED TO

Brandi Cooper

Illustrations by Khantyn Cox

# Dedication

I would like to dedicate this book to all of the pure-hearted people all over the world. Do not let life change you or harden your heart. God made you that way for a reason and a better purpose.

At times, it may seem as though good/genuine people finish last, but we will always finish on top!

To my step dad Sterling Bethea, who always pushed me to be far from mediocre I thank you so much. I do all things in your honor, and I hope you are smiling down on me. Last but most definitely not least, I dedicate every breath I take to God.

Without you Lord I am beyond nothing. Thank you for blessing me with this gift. I vow to use this platform for greatness.

Copyright © Brandi Cooper 2018

All rights reserved. No part of this publication may be reproduced, distributed, or transmitted in any form or by any means, including photocopying, recording, or other electronic or mechanical methods, without the prior written permission of the publisher, except in the case of brief quotations embodied in critical reviews and certain other noncommercial uses permitted by copyright law.

Title: Cocaine
Author: Brandi Cooper
ISBN: 978-0692070550]
Publisher: Level B
Printed in United States of America
First Edition: April 2018
For permission requests, contact the publisher at www.brandicooper.com

Delight yourself in the Lord, and he will give you the desires of your heart."

- Psalm 37:4

# Table of Contents

**PREFACE** ............................................................. 1

**EXPERIMENTATION** .................................... 2

    Sink or swim ................................................................ 4

    Cocaine ........................................................................ 5

    Intuition ......................................................................... 6

    Isaa Wife ....................................................................... 7

    Butterflies ...................................................................... 9

    Honey-moon Stage ................................................... 10

    Home ........................................................................... 12

    Truthfully ..................................................................... 13

**REGULAR USE** ................................................ 14

    Intermission: Tunnel Vision ...................................... 15

    High ............................................................................. 17

    Pathetic ...................................................................... 18

    Intermission: Self Control ........................................ 20

    Delusion ...................................................................... 21

    Feeble ......................................................................... 22

    Intermission: Crazy ................................................... 23

**ABUSE** ............................................................... 24

    Desperate .................................................................. 26

- Intermission: Denial ............................................. 27
- Love is Love ....................................................... 28
- Misinterpretation of Love ..................................... 30
- Purple Hearts ...................................................... 31
- Half Way There ................................................... 32

# DEPENDENCY ............................................. 33

- Scared of change ............................................... 35
- Half Way Gone ................................................... 36
- Intermission: Tables Turn ..................................... 37
- Karma Handle My Lightweight ............................ 38
- Intermission: Changed ........................................ 40
- Empty ................................................................. 41
- Regret ................................................................ 42

# RECOVERY .................................................. 43

- Dancing with the Devil ....................................... 45
- Lust ..................................................................... 46
- Ignorance is Bliss ................................................ 48
- Intermission: P.S. I Still Love You ........................... 50
- Acceptance ........................................................ 51
- Holding on ......................................................... 53
- Intermission: Operation Let Go ............................ 54
- Cancer and Scorpio Link .................................... 56
- Realizations ........................................................ 57

# REHABILITATION ..................................59

    Boys vs. Men............................................61

    Mind vs heart..........................................63

    The Last Laugh........................................65

    The Role...................................................66

    Boys vs Men part 2..................................67

    Nostalgia...................................................69

    My Future Pride and Joy .......................71

# PREFACE

I began crafting poems as an escape from my own reality my freshman year of college. The thought of publishing a book always lingered in the back of my mind, but I hesitated to unveil my most genuine emotions to the world. At that time, only a select few close to me were aware of my identity as a writer. My current drive to share my poetry comes from a desire to offer solace to other young women navigating life's challenges. Remember, you are not alone; pain is an inevitable facet of existence, and its weight diminishes over time.

I chose to entitle this book 'Cocaine' to draw a parallel between the exhilaration and addiction associated with substance abuse and the intense emotions experienced when in love. Love is like a drug. It can be addicting, and even when you know you should quit or move on sometimes you just don't trust that you have the willpower to.

This book is more than me sharing moments of creativity. It is my testimony! I am here to show you that you do have that willpower! Whatever you want in life is attainable. That goes for the lifestyle you desire, the career you envision, and even the spouse of your dreams. The key is to NEVER settle for anything other than what you desire. t

I am not sure what to expect after the release of this book, nor do I have all the answers. I'm proud to admit that I am still growing and still learning to practice what I preach. I am still on my own self-love journey just like every other woman, but I do plan to help others in any way that I can. I have realized that this is a journey, not a destination. A special thanks goes to my family, friends, anyone who has inspired me to be a light for others, and you…the reader! May God bless you all! Feel free to reach out to me, and share your thoughts at www.brandicooper.com

# EXPERIMENTATION

being intrigued by something new so much that you're willing to try it, regardless of the consequences…

## Sink or swim

My love is so deep.

I wonder will I ever find someone who is able to handle it.

Most men drown when they touch me, but somehow, I always end up being the one who dies.

I think it's because they would rather let me drown in myself rather than to learn how to swim with me.

Men appreciate the blueness of my ocean and how clear it is.

Everyone before me has given them the reflections of others.

I'm "different".

They love that when they look into me, they can only see themselves.

It's enticing.

But fear keeps them from swimming deeper.

And rather than learning how to swim with me they let me drown alone while they run back to the shore.

What's more fearless than a man?

## Cocaine

When you touch me, I swear it feels like I deserve you.

I wonder if I do.

I wonder if all the girls before me have felt that same way or if it's just something special between me and you.

I wonder when you touch me…. what do you feel?

Just skin on your skin? Body heat and curves?

Or do you touch me and know that what we have is real?

I hope that you mourn my touch when I'm away.

I hope anxiety creeps down your back when you're not next to me.

Assure me.

Please.

I want to know that you feel it too.

You have shown me that drugs aren't the only thing that people can be addicted to.

## Intuition

I feel him, even when he's not physically here.

This love is so strong that I think he could tell me that he doesn't love me.

And then God and I would laugh and have a conversation about how the love is still there.

This is different…. from anything I've ever known.

I never understood what people meant, when they would say that when you meet that special someone you'll just know.

But right now, I am so sure.

Sometimes I get scared, because what if I'm wrong?

What if I'm just about to lose you?

But then something calms me.

It's like God is telling me for him, Brandi I choose you.

Through adversity I still love him.

Through pain I only want to cling to him more.

Something in him tells me that he's sick, and my love is the only cure.

## Isaa Wife

I don't want to move too fast, but I don't want to move too slow.

How do I find the perfect pace to make this love last long enough to grow?

When you met me, I had scars because of all of the others that I let get too close.

But you gave me hope!

You gave me dreams of things that I never thought could happen for me!

I wanted his and her Benz's, and you suggested a family of three.

I pray for you, and I hope that every night you pray for me.

If you make me happy, I promise to give you the utmost love and loyalty.

I promise you that you'll never find another like me.

One that will stick by your side whether you're right or wrong till infinity.

## Butterflies

I know nothing is perfect, but sometimes I feel like you're the closest thing to perfect I'm ever going to get.

If one day our lives blew in different directions, I know for a fact you're someone I'm never going to forget.

I don't sit around and dream about our wedding or kids running around behind a white picket fence, but if you needed help robbing a bank or rolling a blunt there is no doubt that I'd be with it.

I'm usually the one getting spoiled, but it's something about you that makes me want to spoil you.

And I don't just mean with designer jeans and other material things.

I want to make you happy and amazed that a girl could care this much.

I want you to miss me when I'm away and never be satisfied with another woman's touch.

I'm scared to fall in love with you, it might just be too much for me to deal.

Sometimes I'm not sure if I'm just crazy and over attached, or if I truly have a right to feel the way I feel.

I look at you and I'm happy.

You touch me and my body is on chill.

I know I never want to lose you, but I'll be forever grateful for getting the chance to experience something real.

## Honey-moon Stage

I remember when you were scared to touch me because you didn't want to over step boundaries, and I wanted you to so bad.

The first time we had sex you whispered: "What's wrong?"

Must've shown on my face that I was screaming "Brandi wtf are you doing?!" inside my head.

I still have the picture that you attempted to draw of me the first time I let you sleep over.

And I still know how it felt to kiss you for the first time.

It felt like home.

I remember that you don't like to drink out of straws and that you wash your hands several times a day.

You hate McDonald's and love girls with red hair.

I remember how I use to embarrass you by giving you the hugest hickeys all over your neck or how I would get drunk or high and automatically want you.

I know where you like to be touched and how you like to be licked because I remember all of the first times we had and all the things that we did.

You're like a book that I'll never get tired of reading.

I'm addicted to your life.

You're a puzzle that I would put together over and over again until I found all the different methods to make it right.

You're the first one to make me break every single rule that I set up inside my head.

It's some feelings you just run with

And as soon as I met you that's exactly what I did.

I remember when you were scared to touch me because you didn't want to over step boundaries, and I wanted you to so bad.

And now over a year later, you still give me all those same "first" and all of those same feelings that kept me on edge

## Home

I could tell it was your hands even if you touched me in a pitch-black room.

I could tell it's your lips even if you kissed me while I was blind folded.

I could tell that it was your voice even if I heard a million voices that were louder.

I could tell that you were different but I couldn't tell how.

I was intrigued and captivated.

I wanted to know the stories behind your smile.

From the moment I met you, I could tell that when we got through, I would never be the same all because of you.

## Truthfully

Sometimes he makes moves, and outsiders tell me I should let it go.

I act like I consider their advice, but only I can understand the complexity of him.

I don't expect them to know.

He hasn't been perfect, and I have been far from that too.

But he has accepted me when I was wrong, and as long as God tells me that the love is there, I will accept him too.

Kiss me in my dreams.

Let me feel your heart even when you're not close.

I'm sure that other girls have loved you, but you have to know that I love you the most.

# REGULAR USE
incorporating something into your daily lifestyle whether good or bad for you…

## Intermission: Tunnel Vision

I'm not blind to the fact that what we have is not perfect, and I'll never pretend that it is. It's honestly not even close to it. The feelings are there, but the situation is far from ideal. My love for him has been put to the test many times, and every time it has shown through. I do agree that love is not pain and should never be mistaken for it, but a part of love is endurance. When you love someone it's hard to give up on them. Sometimes the easier task is to just try to make things better. When you're dealing with another person sometimes things just clash and don't go in the direction you wish, but you endure it if the love is worth it in your eyes. I have endured so many things for him both big and minute. There are some things that no one is aware of but US, so what else is there to be afraid of?

## High

I cling to him, even when he shows me, I should let go.

He takes from me, and even when I have nothing else to give, I let him borrow a piece of me to make himself whole.

I feed off his eyes and the way his hands melt on my skin when we sleep.

I wake up, and I watch him leave in hopes that he'll return to me.

But when he doesn't, I deal with it.

And I swallow sad words and exclamation points that I should have the right to say.

But I just cling to him, because I want him to look at me and be happy.

I want to pretend like we're perfect and that everything is okay.

## Pathetic

I keep telling myself that maybe we're just not meant to be, but deep down I'm hoping that right now is just not our time and that we'll get where I want us to be eventually.

I have nightmares of you touching girls that aren't me, and them softening the edges of your heart that I haven't got the chance to reach, and it honestly scares me.

I have tried to throw away feelings for you, and every morning I would wake up and they'd be back at the foot of my bed.

It's a bittersweet feeling to know that you have so much care in your heart for some one that you would forgive them for almost anything they did.

I'm trying to think of a remedy to get over you but it's much easier to smile and think of the reasons why I care for you instead.

I know I should let go and it's pathetic how much I don't want you to leave me.

I have so much to offer so it hurts me that it's not enough for you to only want to be with me.

I would take the stars out of the sky

And walk on water if I thought it would make you happy.

I could have any one I want and here I am wanting you once again and you still won't have me.

It's an ache in my chest and an undying yearning in my soul.

If I never talked to you again, then where would the love go?

I could attempt to give it away, but I'm afraid that wouldn't do.

Months apart has put this idea in my head that no one could compare to you.

I'm addicted to your energy.

It's a shame how it has me stuck.

Meeting you made me happy.

I thought I had finally hit the jack pot and landed on some kind of relationship luck

Other people have touched me but beside you, it doesn't mean much

Sometimes I think I would've never laid down with you that that first time if I knew that loving you would be this rough.

## Intermission: Self Control

I hate that you make me feel so many things. I hate that you can make me feel anything at all. Sometimes I wonder if things are as deep between us as I have come to think or if I'm so deep in lust that I can't think straight. I know for a fact that my heart was some form of heart broken when things crashed between us last summer, and if it were lust, I don't believe it would've felt like that to me. I don't believe that last year I fell in love, but maybe I was on my way to be. I hate to say that out loud because I know you weren't on your way to being in love with me. I feel like you're always going to have the upper hand on me no matter how much I try to trick myself to think otherwise. I'll always care more, I'll always want you more, and I'll always miss you more. It's nothing that I can think of that will ever put us completely on the same page, no words nor actions.

## Delusion

It's 4 in the morning, and I'm thinking of you.

How cliché of me?

I'm wishing I could delete all our memories and wondering how many Xanax it would take me to forget about you.

This is like torture for me sometimes, but other days it's easy as can be.

No one wants to hear me say that I miss you.

I don't even want to say it aloud.

But right now, I really do miss you, baby.

Please bring him back to me.

Life can be a little dull without him.

Peaceful-ness is no longer what I need.

I would take him back right now, yelling at me.

I would take long messages and us arguing outside.

I would take make-up sex and crying every time we have to say good bye.

Is this love? Is this what I'm supposed to feel?

I rather be sad with you than happy with someone else.

## Feeble

A feeling of defeat.

I cried till there wasn't a single tear left in me.

How ironic, because I thought that I was so strong that no one could ever get the best of me.

But when we were done it was nothing left of me.

You didn't even have to try though.

I broke my own heart and brought myself to my own demise though.

I used to think I was so strong

I never thought I would be the broken-hearted girl relating to every love song.

## Intermission: Crazy

I find it crazy how the most important factor of a relationship is to genuinely care about someone and that it is still not enough to keep two people together. It's crazy how someone can hurt you so bad that you feel like you will never feel better all by just living their life. Oh my god, just the thought of this someone touching another makes you sick to your stomach! Thinking about them creating memories with someone else makes you want to cry a river! It's crazy that you can end up hating someone you use to feel like you'd do anything for. I have to act like I don't know someone I fell asleep and woke up next to countless times. It's crazy.

# ABUSE

participating in the constant engagement of something negative despite the risk or connotations associated with this thing…

## Desperate

Dear God, why doesn't he appreciate me?

I love him and it shows.

I cry myself to sleep at night, and I wake up and still love him in the morning.

I'm in love with a man whose heart is cold.

He finds emotions weak, and he thinks being in love is just something you do for fun.

Dear God, why doesn't he love me like he needs me?

I NEED him!

## Intermission: Denial

It's very clear that being done with you is not something that I'm ready for. I have more than enough reasons to say forget you, but I never do because right now I just can't. When I'm ready to be done I'll be done, but until that day this is just what it is. I'm not about to try to force myself to be over you and end up miserable. I figure we've come this far, and if I just tried to forget a person, I care more about than a lot of people, then that wouldn't even make sense. Those months we spent apart speak words to me because my feelings never subsided, and we came back together and made an even stronger connection. I just don't see how it's meant for me to let go. All I can do at this point is love you and care for you in the best ways that I know how and try to not let petty things get in between and hope that it's enough in the end. If it is not, I will cross that bridge when we get to it which I'm praying will be never.

This is not me rewarding your wrong doings because you are wrong as hell a lot of times, and this is also not me pointing the finger at you or trying to make you feel bad about that. After all, I am the one who accepts you when you're wrong every single time, and I take no shame in that. If I made you feel low for being wrong, I'm just as worst because I constantly accept it from you. I'm doing this strictly for me because caring about you makes me happy, and I'm not going to pretend like leaving you alone is going to be easy for me and that it's something I'm ready for when it isn't.

## Love is Love

He won't let go.

And I guess some part of me must like that attention.

He says we just have this crazy addictive love, where the word "goodbye" could never be mentioned.

He says that every time I open up, he'll be the one at my door.

He also points out that I'm special, and no one has ignited a fire in him like this before.

Every time I give him a part of me, he always wants more.

It's scary for two people to love each other this way.

Pledging allegiance to someone's heart has a history of leaving people in dismay.

But he has been there many times to wipe my tears away.

Even when I am hurting, he has the power to make me hopeful that everything will be okay.

And that there's no reason why I shouldn't continue to stay.

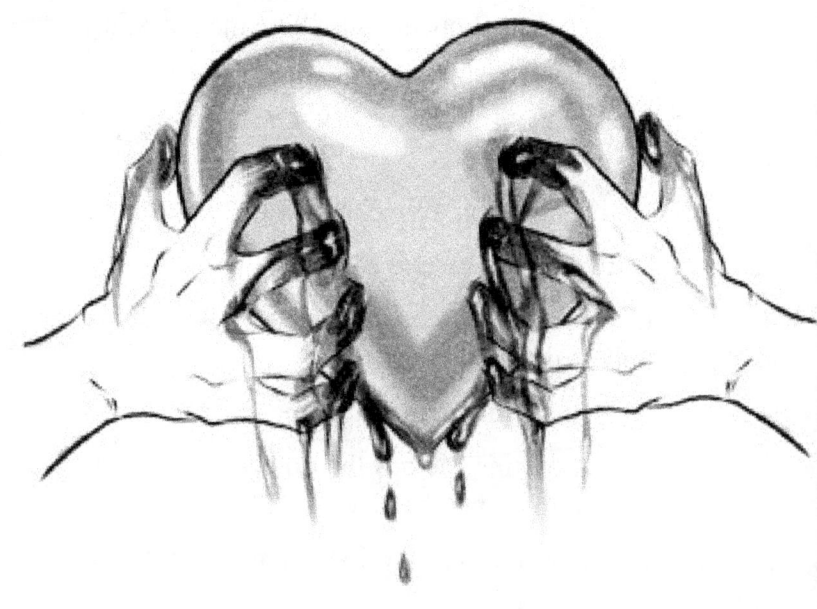

## Misinterpretation of Love

He says he loves me.

But we both know nothing about love.

Sometimes I feel like I need him.

When I'm sobbing and going crazy only us being right can put me back together again.

He says he cares.

That he appreciates me, even though it is hard for him to show at times.

I am patient.

I am understanding.

I pray for him even when I feel like I hate him.

Some days I wear my heart on my sleeve, and I hide it well.

Other days my emotions seep through unconsciously.

I love him.

But we both know nothing about love.

## Purple Hearts

They say that if you lose love, and it comes back then it means so much more.

Which makes me wonder, if you lose it twice then what was it even all for?

What was the point of us coming back together for us to just not work out again?

I'm tired, but I'm not ready to raise my white flag up and let this be the end.

I want it to work so badly.

I want us to be happy, just you and me.

If I had the power to knock down every obstacle that came our way, only God knows where we would be.

Why everything has to be so complicated is something I just can't understand.

But do I choose to move on, or just hope we're at the finish line holding hands at the end?

## Half Way There

I wish that love was enough to make things feel perfect how I believe they should be

I wish I could erase memories of you hurting me in ways you've promised would never be.

I wish god could come down and tell me why I had to meet you at all.

And why do I have to allow you to hurt me to show you that I'm giving you my all?

Why do I have to go insane to prove to you that the love is there?

And once that's done, I have to strip down my heart just to show you… you also have a place in there

I want you to stand by my side, even when I'm not there physically

Love me how I love you

Don't hurt me then claim it's meant to be

I just want to be in love and be happy with the decision I made.

Now a days it seems like the more I love you, the closer I feel like I am to my grave.

When it comes to you, I'm ashamed of the way I behave.

All I know is that when I'm dying, you loving me is the only way I feel I can be saved.

# DEPENDENCY

having withdrawals when you feel like you cannot get to this "thing" and/or feeling as though you are unable to survive without it…

## Scared of change

It's scary to let go of someone you love
No matter what they do to you
You want to try to fix it
But some things become unfixable

It's scary to let go of someone you love
And to try and find someone new
Will they touch me how you did?
And make me feel as good as you?

I'm scared to wake up and miss you
Or to daydream about something you once said
Moving on would be much easier if I could just get you out of my head

It's scary to give up on someone you love
To move on and say goodbye
When winning their heart was the goal, and you have to give up on your prize
I love you…. I do

And it is so scary to let go of you.
But it's even scarier to hold on to a love that hurts me the way that you do.

## Half Way Gone

I hate you.

You make me sick!

You poison everything I let you touch.

While I just go behind you and try to "fix" it

I f*cking love you!

Do you get that?

I cannot fathom that you do.

Do I have to kill myself physically to show you that you are killing me mentally?

What do I have to do, so you won't choose to hurt me?

Just be with me!

Just love me how I love you…please!

Protect the love that you've planted inside of me.

It must boost your ego, to be loved unconditionally and not have to live righteously.

Appreciate me how you do when you feel like I'm half way out of your life.

You have promised to one day marry me, but I don't believe that pain should be the entry of becoming a wife.

## Intermission: Tables Turn

How could you? How could you? How could you? How could you? ……HOW COULD YOU TREAT ME LIKE THIS??? You know I don't deserve this! You don't just wake up and decide to treat people like nothing just because you have the option to! I love you, and you know that!! You can tell yourself whatever you want that justifies you treating me this way. You can try to convince yourself of whatever helps you sleep at night, but deep down you know exactly what you're doing to me. You felt my love even when I thought I was doing a good job at concealing it, and now you pretend as if those days never existed. You will reap what you've sewn. You will feel what you've given. You will be sucked dry where you've been replenished. Forgive him father, for he does not know what he has done. Tables always turn.

# Karma Handle My Lightweight

Have you ever prayed to God to take the love away?

Or woke up in the middle of the night and thought about him and had to tell yourself that eventually everything will be okay?

Have you ever compared memories of the past to how he ended up treating you?

I've learned that when you give a man too much, he will treat you like he never needed you.

You can say that I don't love you.

You can say that I'm just a user.

You can say whatever justifies things...whatever convinces you, "yeah I should do this to her."

But we both know the truth.

You're a coward, that is running from what's real.

So instead, you put the blame on me and choose to disregard how I feel.

You love me today and will convince yourself that I'm disloyal next.

I've told you sorry for things I shouldn't be sorry for

And instead of appreciation, you try to hang it around my neck.

You will regret the day you used me.

You will regret the day you refused to listen.

You will regret the day you shunned me out of your life as soon as that karma kicks in.

You will love a woman, but she won't love you more.

You will open your heart to her beyond measure, and she will be the one to close the door.

There will be many women around you, but you will never be content.

When you think you've found a wife, she will still act like a girlfriend.

You will wonder what's wrong with this world.

Why can't you find a good woman?

And then Brandi will pop into your head, and you will remember the day you decided it was time to treat her like nothing.

## Intermission: Changed

Everything comes back to you. I used to think I was such a good judge of character, but dealing with you has even made me mistrustful of myself. My judgment is no longer 100% because of you. I usually see warning signs, but with you, I saw nothing. How will I ever learn to trust myself again, let alone someone else?

## Empty

He used to lie in a way that made me never think to question his words.

And sometimes he spoke about love as if he knew what it was all about.

He had the power to make me feel lucky to have him but also cursed to have met him in the same sense.

And I believe that only someone who has loved him before would understand that.

He has looked at me in the day time with eyes that have made me feel like we belong together, and then he would fall asleep next to eyes that I didn't own at night.

I have experienced the joyfulness of being in his good grace and the emptiness of being sucked dry by his actions.

It makes no sense how I could be in a room full of people that really love me

And still not feel a thing… all because of him.

## Regret

I still think about you sometimes.

And I'm still in awe at the memories I made with the man I met compared to the person you've more recently shown yourself to be.

How could someone be so wrong and live with themselves?

If it weren't for me falling asleep on your chest many of nights, I would question if you even had a heart.

My body doesn't feel the same knowing that I let someone like you touch it so many times.

You are cold and dirty, to say the least.

But what does that say about me?

How could I ever find it in me to love a person like that?

# RECOVERY

understanding the behavior that led to abuse and learning how to create your own self-sufficient happiness...

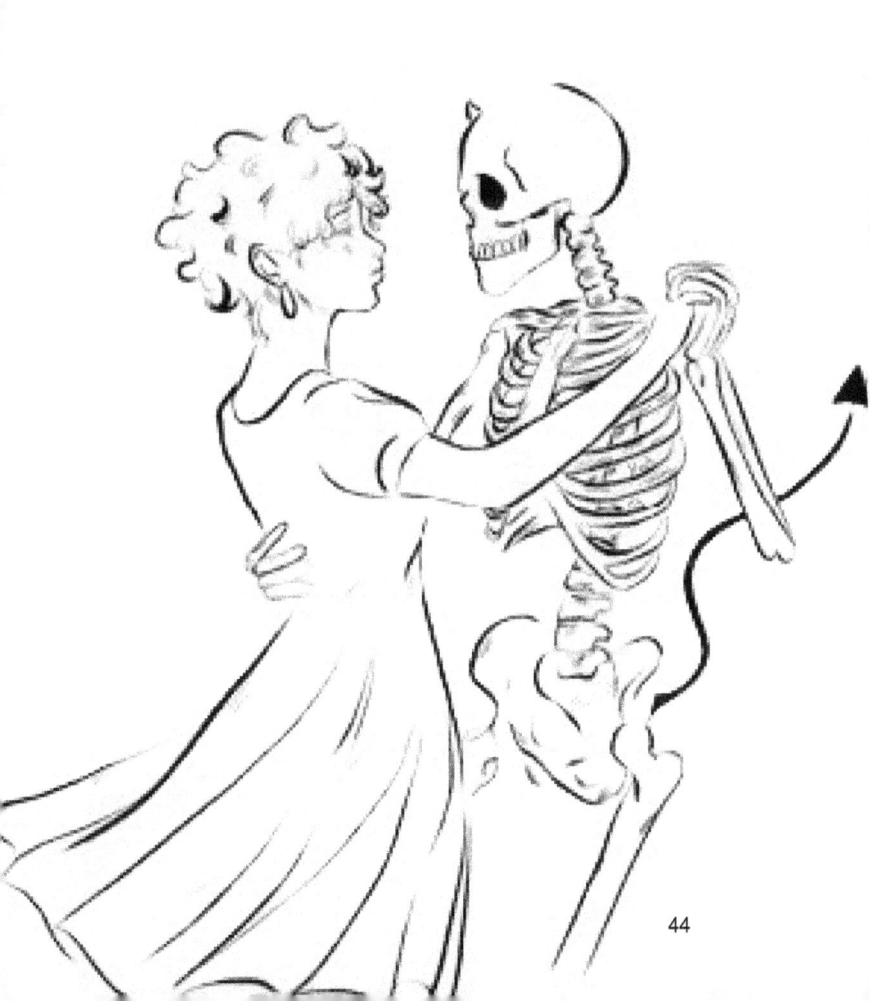

## Dancing with the Devil

What is it about you that makes me stay when I should go?

Makes me say yes when I know I should be saying no.

Puts me on a high, then brings me down to a low.

I don't know because you never hesitated to be hurtful to me

But I still longed for the other side of you

The person you pretended to be

Even though the real you was staring at me, the other side of you was as strong as can be

Taking control, apparently.

It could be possible that the affection had my mind gone.

Science says that sex brings out emotions in women that make attachments strong.

It could be possible that your words were just that sweet

When I met you my heart was shattered, and sometimes you made me feel like I was getting back that missing piece.

It could be possible that I was just being dumb.

I knew the right thing to do, but to the wrong…I'd run.

It's crazy to realize that something that felt so real just turned out to be for fun.

Sometimes I wish everything between us could just be undone.

I thought I knew how to play the game, but in the end, you still won.

## Lust

Bittersweet.

It's so wrong, but it still tastes good to me.

I want to hate you, but you're so deep in my system that it's hard to shake you.

You could never understand though

It's not love, but things got deeper than we planned though

If life was perfect you probably would've been my man though

But in reality, what we had never stood a chance though.

Innocent intentions led to something so passionate that I didn't want to think about ending

The thought of us quitting use to paint a picture of sadness, so vivid

Others could never understand because they were never there to witness

Why I'm so attached

Why it's hard to fall back

Why it feels like we're in sync so much that we can't realize that we really don't match

You were always so hot and cold

You just could never make your mind up

Which led to me being stuck

And even though all of your actions told me to give it up it just wasn't enough

And now that's it's over, I don't know how I should feel

I'm thinking I will never be one of those girls that luck up and finds something real

I'm left with a lesson learned and a couple of feelings I'm just ready to burn because I gave a piece of me away to someone that didn't earn

But I'll take us as an experience

You showed me that the fakest people can still come off so genuine

## Ignorance is Bliss

I wish I would've never got to know that a person like you exist.

You touched my mind and my body and it left me powerless.

To me, your flaws are stitched together so perfectly.

So, I know losing this feeling is going to bring out the worst in me.

Even with your wrong doings, I try to find ways to make them right.

Even when I want to scream "NO!" I only have the strength to whisper, "I might".

You have magic at your fingertips.

When you touch me my mind melts.

God has got to be in you because this feeling couldn't be produced by anyone else.

With you, I feel waves of emotions.

I'm an anchor drowning in the sea.

If you told me that people could fly and that animals could talk, then I swear to God that is what I would believe.

I'm naïve for you.

I'm a child, and you're my favorite super hero.

You give me a little bit of guidance.

I'm like a flower that you're holding in your hand.

Other boys tell me I'm a rose and that I'm beautiful but see you, you like dandelions.

How you could not want the most wanted flower of them all is something I will never understand.

But I guess you just wanted to pick me and smell me; not plant me in your own garden.

## Intermission: P.S. I Still Love You

After all this time, my feelings still mean nothing to you. I'm in love, and you don't care. You're immune to all my tears even though you say your love for me is there. I drive you crazy, and you break my heart. Stay content with the decisions you've made because this is the end baby. I'm too good for you…. the only truth you've ever spoken to me.

## Acceptance

I heard that settling was so 2013.

But when you give up on love does that certify that it wasn't worth a thing?

I have moved mountains in your honor and hurt myself to try and keep "us" safe.

I've tried to build bridges to get over it, but I realized man made attributes cannot stop nature from taking its place.

And surely, I cannot fight the universe or get in the way of fate

Right now, is just not our time, a reality that I'm accepting but that I still hate.

I've been told not to say that I deserve better,

Because that would mean that you deserve better too.

And ironically when I think about better, I only think about bringing out the best in you.

Because what's better about someone treating me so well and still wishing it was you?

What's better about making someone fall in love with me and knowing that my heart still lies with you?

"Move on," they say, "because girl you can do so much better".

But they've never talked to you, seen you through my eyes, or woken up next to you and felt your skin on their skin and instantly became wetter.

They've never had a man who made them want to pick up a book and enroll in a class or two.

All for the cause of being better and not just for me but for him too.

I am forever moved by him, and I feel that I was blessed to get a chance to experience his energy.

And even though our current state leaves me unhappy, I find peace in knowing that what's meant to be is what's meant to be.

I have come to terms with the fact that all great romances do not come with a certification that that person is the one

And just like seasons, feelings fade and things change and we must adjust and prepare for new ones.

There is some sick beauty in loving someone through pain and a positive aspect in the art of letting go.

There is a such thing as smiling through thunderstorms and being happy in the midst of sorrow, and there is a way to be content when you feel like you are ready to love someone but fate and the universe say "no".

# Holding on

2013 is over, and I believe that my longing for you is too.

Around this time last year, we were first meeting.

So new and intrigued.

Trying to forget you and hold on at the same time has been so hard to do.

I have almost completely let the flower die that you watered in my mind.

I remember when I could still feel us laying together, and how our hands interlocked at the perfect times.

Us talking until one of us was quiet enough to kiss, or getting high and melting into each other.

Feeling you breathe on my neck and how we both did it with passion.

And how you sucked every smile from me and made all our great moments bitter memories that you left me all alone to deal with in the spring

I have written so much about you, and you still haven't read a thing.

## Intermission: Operation Let Go

I don't know when I became so forgiving, or what exact day that it was when I woke up and you owned such a big piece of my heart. It's like I never really knew how much I cared about you until you started to hurt me. I don't know when things began to switch around, and I loved you more than you loved me. You reminded me that people are still willing to abuse the power that they beg for. The very thing that they once felt like they would do anything to obtain could be the same thing they treat with no value. You showed me that love can be a mind game.

If you don't make the perfect move at the perfect time you can lose the person you think is perfect for you. I'm making new memories with other people, but I still can't erase our old ones. I still remember everything...down to the first time we kissed.

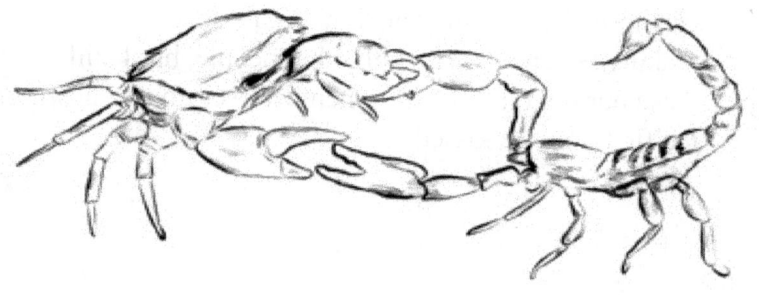

## Cancer and Scorpio Link

Everything I didn't want to happen between us, still happened.

All the hurt I constantly ran away from still landed inside of me.

The short end of the stick that I tried to give to you at times still landed in my hands.

I wish that we could've met at a time later on.

When I was more content with the pain that life has shown to me, and when life humbled you more.

Even with tears in my eyes, my vision is clear enough to always see you.

I hope that one day we will bloom together again.

Maybe one day in the future we'll wake up together, and I'll get to watch the sun rise on your cheeks how I used to.

I could never really hate you like I say I do.

## Realizations

I've given you loyalty that right now you don't have the mental capacity to appreciate.

But still… you are the one that asked for it.

You look at me now, and see beauty that no longer moves you.

Ironically, to you I use to be everything.

He used to fantasize about sleeping next to me, and every time I came around, he always made sure to show his best for me.

But I've noticed that perspective changes once you get everything you want.

At that point, there's no need for a front.

And of course, like many women…I become the fool that can never let go or accept what has become of us.

And I have to rearrange my mind about a person who promised they were someone I could trust.

I think a part of me is addicted to pain.

Every time I told myself to stay inside, I still walked to the thunderstorm and tried to dance with the rain.

Every time you made me cry, it only watered my love for you more.

Again, and again I bring this flower back hoping you will appreciate my unwavering devotion.

Only to have you laugh and yank the flower from its roots because you know it will grow again.

I had to ask myself: What's more ungrateful than an entitled boy dressed up as a man who knows you love unconditionally?

# REHABILITATION
a complete cease of abusive/dependent behavior, entering life with a new outlook that prevents the relapse of abuse...

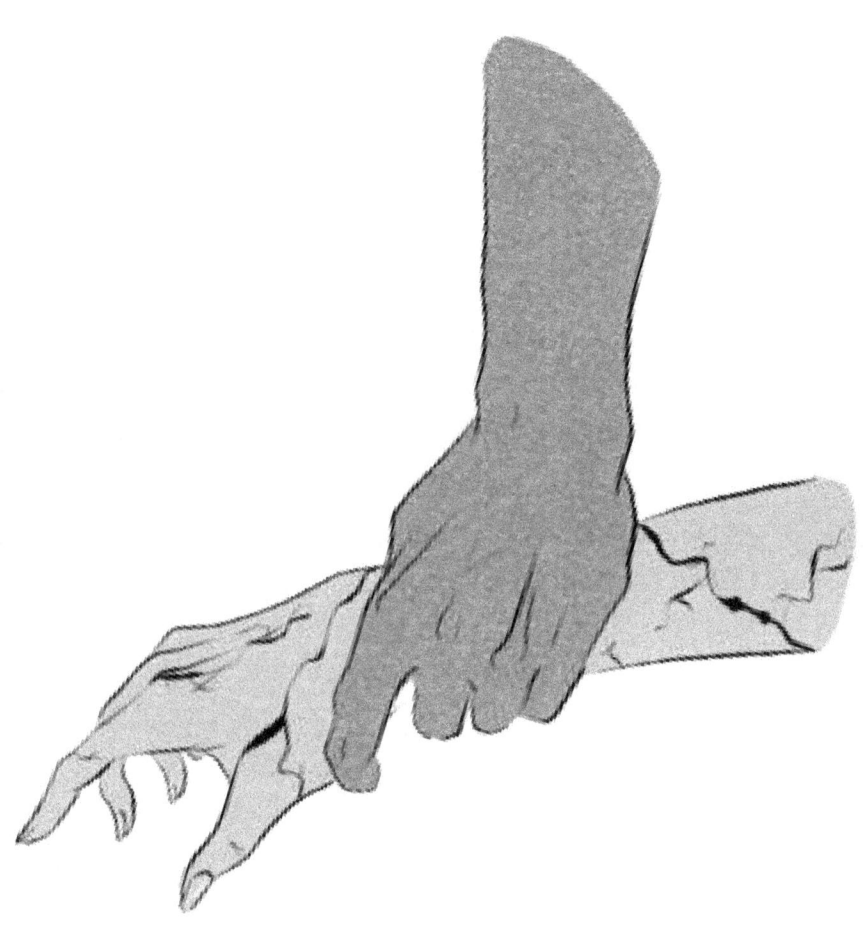

# Boys vs. Men

I met a boy.

We would talk, and I was always honest and he loved me.

He knew my flaws, and he noticed everything that I didn't love about myself.

And it only made him want me more.

When I finally got ready to love him back, he left me.

And at that moment we both realized that my love was too pure.

In August, I met a boy.

I had stuff in me that my body wasn't ready for, and when I stumbled, he didn't let me fall.

I was sad so I let him hug and kiss me too soon.

I felt wrong and I was ashamed, but I still decided to let him touch me some more.

He was bad for me but I was already attached, so he kept me stuck.

He would shoot me down.

And when it looked like I was about to die he would cry over my body, and nurse me back to health.

He tried to taint my love, and poison my mind with thoughts that other pure lovers didn't exist anymore.

I finally told myself he didn't care, and I moved on.

In January, a boy caught my attention with his words, but we chose each other for different reasons.

I was so intrigued that I broke my own rules for him.

He didn't even have to ask.

He treated me good, and my heart swelled with emotion and feelings for him.

Every night we laid together.

And I would let him touch me.

Because he did it the best!

And I thought I deserved him and a sample of what passion could be like.

I was a lot but I wanted to be more…. for him.

Too good to be true is what I told him he seemed to be.

He kissed me.

And he laughed.

And he assured me feelings were mutual.

And I never had to worry.

Time went on and without trying he showed me that I had come to another dead end.

But I still wanted to kiss and lay with him at night to make myself feel like seasons and months could rewind.

I was hoping I could wake up and we would be back in January again.

In May and June, I woke up with sadness in my heart that not even sleep could evade.

I had decided to give up on meeting a boy in August because I realized I had to meet myself.

I realized I had to fall for my own words and that one day a man will come along and fall for them too.

## Mind vs heart

Today I kissed someone else with lips that feel like they belong to you

And I let him touch me and his hands melted in the same spots where yours used to

I felt bad

As he kissed me, all I could think about was you.

I have given you love, that you aren't mature enough to think through.

Even with your disregard, my heart still pledges allegiance to you.

But I realized, you do not own me.

The places where your hands met my skin do not belong to you.

Every curve and every corner belong to me, not to you.

And if you deserved it, I would never have to question if you do.

## The Last Laugh

I hope you look for me in everyone that you meet

And that you have to take a quick sigh in the morning when she rolls over, and you realize it isn't me.

I know she touches you but it is not like me.

I know she kisses you but it is not like me.

I know she gives to you but you still wish you were taking it from me.

You are a fool and I am content.

I've lost a nuisance, and you've lost your only win.

I've gained happiness while you live a mediocre life with your new girlfriend.

## The Role

I've met many men like you.

Males that think that women are just bath tubs to soak their egos in.

Beings created solely for the purpose of enhancing male existence.

Men that do not realize the beautiful curse placed upon us immediately when the Lord allows us to open our eyes.

We are made from the rib of a man, but everyday a woman gives a piece of her to mend another.

A woman is expected to be a nurturer even before she becomes a mother.

A woman is expected to cook and clean even before she has a ring.

A woman is expected to live life with an open forgiving heart and give even when she feels she has nothing.

She knows the world would look down upon her if she couldn't turn nothings into beautiful somethings.

Well, what kind of woman would you be?

If you weren't able to carry the weight of the world on your shoulders, and still smile in the morning while fixing your man's tea?

## Boys vs Men part 2

In December 2016 I met a man…who vowed to treat my heart with care, but I was still afraid.

I had already taught myself how to be less attached, less loyal, and just less of a lover.

In my mind, those were the traits that gave others the upper hand and held me back.

Those were the traits that people take from you and never give back.

Those were the traits that other people want from you, but yet they lack.

This man would always assure me "Brandi, it's just you and me!"

And in the back of my mind, I'd be thinking "hmmm, the last boy said the same thing."

We would spend days together at a time, and he would tell me "baby you're the one!"

And I'd be thinking well, "I'm sure he still has 4, 5, and 6, but I'm just his favorite type of fun."

Some nights I would lay next to this man and show him tiny pieces of my heart and that showed my warmness.

Some nights I would stare at this man and we both could feel my heart smiling and that showed my admiration.

Some nights this man would touch me and my heart would start racing and that showed my addiction for him.

But some days I would call and never come or he'd call and I'd never pick up and that showed that I was detached.

Some days I would entertain a guy that means nothing to me and he'd find out and that showed my disloyalty.
Some days he would want to work it out and I would disregard him, and it showed that I was less of a lover.
I would pick up the relationship and put it down when I wanted.
I would kiss him till we both ran out of breath and then disappear the next morning...until one day he had enough.
I came back hoping he'd love me again but he said that he was fed up.
He said, "I want a girl who is a real lover, one that is loyal, and shows that she cares."
And that's when I truly realized I had made a mistake
I had confused a man that wanted to replenish me for another boy that just wanted to take.

## Nostalgia

I'm sorry that I am so hard to love

But in my mind, I have visions of us that you could never dream of

I think about making you happy.

I close my eyes and all I could see is your smile.

And then I wake up with sadness because I realize you aren't here with me now.

Our memories keep me up at night, I go to sleep with the taste of you on my tongue

I have tried to throw my feelings away, and then again blossoms a new one.

And it hurts, ----cause' I know I'm the one that's constantly dimming our light.

I remember every way you've shown you care, so I must accept that you're not willing to do so more than twice.

And if I could go back in time I just might.

To lay in bed and listen to Sade with you.

I know you remember those nights.

And now I'm filled with regret because I want to do everything more than right.

I wish that you would just call me right now and say, "Baby come be with me!".

I wish that when you went to sleep tonight that I'm in your dreams and all you could see is me.

I wish that I wasn't so complicated so you could really understand how I feel.

I run and I hide from you because my feelings are very genuine and real.

I'm afraid to be hurt and I'm afraid to feel pain, so I run away to conceal it.

And I always hope that I can come back and you still feel the same.

And I know that love is not a game, but sometimes I test the strength of relationships to see who will leave me and who will remain.

## My Future Pride and Joy

To my unborn daughter, I'd say, love yourself first!!

So that even when it feels like he doesn't it will not be the end of your world.

Put yourself first, and be selfish with your time.

Never let someone make you feel like being this way is a bad thing.

If you ever see a man disrespect a woman, never find it funny.

He is not caught up in the moment that is his character, and it might be you next.

Run in the opposite direction!

Look in the mirror and realize that you are beautiful.

You were born that way.

Do not allow someone else to notice the unique shape of your eyes before you do.

Be flattered but never addicted to compliments.

Make God a priority in your life and never put the average man on a pedestal where God should be.

All men are flawed but he.

Be wise when choosing people, make sure people are around you for the right reasons and that you share the same values as them.

If you are ever uncomfortable remove yourself from that situation, and never deal with people who make you feel such a way.

Give people chances, but be aware of their faults.

It is okay to cry, but when you find yourself crying over the same thing know that there is something going on that you need to change.

Do not cry yourself to sleep at night, and then smile at me in the morning.

I am here for you.

I already love you so much and I don't even know when we are ever going to meet.

# To women all across the world

I love you! Trust me, life has handed me more obstacles than people of the opposite sex lying to me. Like many, that has only been one among many things that have contributed to the disruption of my happiness.

This book is a dramatization of my past emotions, and served as a creative outlet from reality to some extent. I pray that you find that outlet. I pray that you find that career path. I pray that you are carried to your destiny, and that you see a light for yourself at the end. I pray that you do not relish in unhappiness, and let the devil distract you from your true purpose.

I am your sister, your cousin, your friend, and I want to see you win! Always take control of the things you are able to in your life, and never let the rest worry you. You can be the master of your future or the assistant to your own demise. Always be wise and pray constantly.

♥ Brandi Cooper ♥

God sent two wise women my way that told me to always remember that women are engines, not anchors! Respect us!

www.ingramcontent.com/pod-product-compliance
Lightning Source LLC
Chambersburg PA
CBHW070208100426
42743CB00013B/3092